Table of Contents

Getting Started

Cupcake cakes, also called "pull-apart cakes," are quickly becoming a favorite of kids and adults alike. Fun to make, easy to serve and exciting to eat, a cupcake cake requires no cutting, forks or plates. Cupcakes can be made and frozen ahead of time, making final preparation a breeze. Purchased decorating icing can make them even simpler to make.

There is room for the creative individual as well. Choose your own bases, candy decorations, decorative baking cup liners, and other details to make your cakes unique. Once you have made a cute cupcake cake from these pages, you will see just how easy it can be.

How to...

Create a serving base for cupcake cakes: There are many options for serving bases, but the key is to choose a sturdy base that will support a heavy cake, be the right size for the cupcake arrangement and complement the cake's design.

Serving base ideas include cardboard or inverted baking sheets or jelly roll pans covered with fabric, tissue paper or decorative paper such as scrapbooking pages or gift-wrap. Plastic food covering, especially the type that seals when pressed, can be wrapped over the fabric or paper cover to prevent grease spots from developing under the cupcakes. Other easy ideas for bases which do not require covering include a pizza stone or a large pretty platter. If a large cake is planned, use a large poster frame which has a built-in "finished" edge; just place the fabric or pretty paper under the plastic cover and secure it as you would a poster.

Cupcake
Cakes

Easy
Pull-apart cakes
make parties fun!

Printed in the United States of America
by G&R Publishing Co.

Published By:

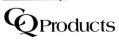

507 Industrial Street
Waverly, IA 50677

ISBN-13: 987-156383-363-2
ISBN-10: 1-56383-363-8
Item #7047

Bake the cupcakes: Paper or foil baking cup liners, not only help with pan clean-up after baking, they can add a decorative element to your cupcake cake creation. Many varieties, such as polka dots, stripes and an assortment of colorful paper and foil cups are available in grocery stores, kitchen and hobby shops or from on-line venders. Examples of how baking cup liners can enhance the final look of the cupcake cake can be found with Hickory Dickory Dock on p. 18 and Fit for a Princess on p. 28.

When measuring batter, carefully fill each baking cup evenly so cupcakes will be the same level after baking. After they are baked, be sure they are fully cooled before frosting and decorating. Cupcakes freeze nicely and thaw quickly, making final preparations less time consuming.

Cupcakes can be baked in three different sizes, each requiring different baking pans and various-sized baking cups. Be sure to adjust baking times for pan sizes and partial batches to avoid over- or under-baking. Recipes vary; however a general guideline for an 18.25 oz. box mix baked at 350° follows:

60-72 Mini size (approx. 1¾″ - 2″)	=	**11-14 minutes**
22-24 Standard size (approx. 2½″ - 2¾″)	=	**18-22 minutes**
12 Jumbo size (approx. 3″ - 3½″)	=	**19-24 minutes**

Watch cupcakes closely and test for doneness by inserting a clean toothpick into the cupcake near the center and removing it. There shouldn't be uncooked batter or wetness on the toothpick. If there are small crumbs sticking to the toothpick, they are done and not over-baked.

SPECIAL NOTE

Tubes of decorating icing have been listed in whole-tube quantities. Often, leftover icing will be available for a future project. Read manufacturer's instructions for storage suggestions. In general, the required quantities for canned frosting or cups of icing are more specific within the directions for each project.

Decorate the Cake

Arrange the cooled cupcakes on the base as the first step, even if cupcakes will be handled individually while decorating. This helps ensure the appropriate size of the base, number of cupcakes required and general outline and position of the finished cake.

There are two main methods for frosting cupcake cakes. The suggested method for each example is due to the specific design.

1. Smooth icing over the entire cupcake cake design, using an offset spatula and working in broad sweeping strokes, allowing icing to cover the joints between cupcakes. Be sure to place cupcakes snugly against one another. Thicker icing is best to assure it does not sink into the cupcake joints. This method works well for a smooth, solid cake design. *See examples on pages 10 and 24.*

2. Generously frost individual cupcakes and then press them next to one another to form the larger shape of the cake. This method works well when the round shape of the cupcakes is an important element in the final design of the cake. *See examples on pages 16 and 30.*

Pre-filled, purchased decorating icing tubes and pouches with tips or decorating pouches filled with icing and fitted with tips are required for many of the cakes. They are easy and fun to use and will give your creations a professional appearance. Follow the simple manufacturer's instructions for assembling the pouch with the coupler and tip. The most common tips are round or star shaped in small, medium and large sizes. With these tips, you can create dots, lines and borders for the examples shown in this book.

Suggestions for ease and success

- **Small dab of icing under the cupcake:**
  To hold cupcakes in position on the cake base, place a small spot of icing on the bottom of the cupcake's paper or foil baking cup liner and press it gently but firmly into position.
  This is especially important if the base is somewhat slippery or if using mini cupcakes.

- **Non-circular shape:** Since the round shape of a circle can sometimes be limiting to the design of the cake, cupcakes can be cut into halves or quarters and be assembled with whole cupcakes. Be sure to place them with the cut side inward so the paper on the outside matches the other cupcakes. Use a bread knife to slice them for an even cut; carefully cut through the paper as well.

- **Gaps between cupcakes:** When large gaps are not filled in with pieces of cupcake, spaces can be filled with large candy pieces such as chocolates or gumdrops to prevent icing from sinking. This is especially helpful when using canned frosting (not "decorating" icing) from the bakery aisle.

- **Rounded vs. flat-topped cupcakes:** Rounded tops on cupcakes can sometimes make a smooth, flat finish to the cake more challenging. One remedy is to skim off the tops from cupcakes with a bread knife. Instructions indicate when this adjustment was made on sample cakes.

- **Paper patterns:** For complicated patterns or to make more perfect shapes, such as circles, cut patterns from freezer or waxed paper to place on the cake.

- **Toothpick dragging/marking:** Use a toothpick to draw the pattern into the cake icing to provide guidelines for piping icing details.

- **Plastic food storage bags for piping:** When a round decorating tip is required, use a small plastic food storage bag for quick and easy clean-up. Just spoon icing into the bag, smooth it to one corner, twist the top of the bag shut, and snip the tip of the bag's corner to create the round piping tool.

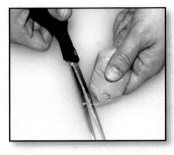

- **Scrape or lift away mistakes:** Icing is somewhat forgiving when it comes to mistakes. If you are not pleased with the first results, icing (especially piped décor) can sometimes be gently scraped from the cake with an offset spatula or lifted away with a toothpick. If at first you don't succeed...

- **Food coloring gels/paste:** To create very bright colored icing, use food coloring gels or paste, rather than traditional liquid food coloring. Gels and pastes are available in unique colors such as black, violet and neon hues.

- **Icing vs. frosting:** Frosting and icing are terms that can be used interchangeably in most cases. For the purposes of this book, icing more commonly refers to a frosting with a stiffer consistency, generally better for decorating purposes. The homemade recipes are referred to as icing.

- **Purchased frosting/icing:** The familiar 12 oz. containers of cake frosting, whipped or creamy, are readily available in the grocery store. They are smooth and creamy and work well for some decorating techniques. The softer "whipped" variety provides a unique look, but will not hold its shape well when piped. The best success for piping decorations is found when using "decorating" icings which are stiffer in consistency, allowing them to retain their shape after application. Decorating icing can be purchased in 16 oz. or 5 lb. containers. A recipe for Bright-White Decorating Icing is on p. 58.

- **Ready–to–use tubes and pouches of colored decorating icing:** Sometimes rich colors are difficult to achieve even with the gels or pastes. Black and red are two examples of colors which are best achieved by purchasing already-tinted icing in tubes or pouches. The screw-on decorating tips make this icing quick and easy to use. Simply knead them before adding the tips for a smoother application.

- **Cover icing when not in use:** Sometimes the decorating process will require icing to be set aside momentarily while applying a different color or technique. Cover icing with a damp cloth or paper towel while not in use to prevent lumping. Cover it with an airtight lid and refrigerate for longer storage.

- **Icing consistency:** If icing is very stiff, bring it to room temperature and whip it briskly. If it continues to be stiff, beat in a drop or two of water.

- **Piping an individual cupcake:** When topping a cupcake with a continuous stream of icing, start at the outside and pipe in a circular pattern to the middle of the cupcake.

- **String/dental floss:** Use cooking string or dental floss to make straight lines across frosted cupcakes, marking the location for piping a different color on top. Gently lay string across the frosted cupcakes and pull gently downward into the icing.

- **Filling iced outlines:** To fill in a shape with icing after piping the outline of the design, dab icing into the middle and use a toothpick to pull frosting to spread it to an outlined edge

- **Tie-dye effect:** Place two different colors of icing into a decorating bag for piping to achieve a tie-dyed blend of colored icing.

- **Smooth a rough icing surface:** To create a smooth finish to decorator icing, lay waxed paper over the semi-set surface and roll gently over the top of it with a rolling pin; carefully peel away the waxed paper.

- **Rough-up a smooth icing surface:** To create an evenly rough finish to icing, wrap plastic food wrap around your hand, or lightly crumple it in your hand, and lightly dab repeatedly over the surface. *See examples on pages 24 and 32.*

Old Glory

You will need
- 16 x 20″ covered serving base
- Small (2″ to 2½″) star cookie cutter

Cupcakes
- 35 standard cupcakes, in red foil liners
  *Example used 2 (18.25 oz.) box mixes, yielding
  44 to 48 standard cupcakes.*

Frosting and décor
- 2½ (16 oz.) containers ready-to-use white frosting
- 3 (6 oz.) pouches red decorating icing with tips
- 3 (6 oz.) pouches white decorating icing with tips
- 1 (6 oz.) pouch blue decorating icing with tip

Directions

Place cooled cupcakes on serving base according to diagram, then remove the nine cupcakes which will make up the star portion of the cake and set aside. Add a small dab of frosting to the bottom of each remaining cupcake to secure it to the base. Spread white frosting over the cupcakes that make up the red and white striped portion of the cake, making it smooth.

With a toothpick, mark the five stripes of the flag into the frosting, using the width of the cupcakes as a guide. Fit a red decorating icing pouch with a medium star tip. Pipe a row of stars along the bottom edge of the flag, from one side to the other. When the first row is complete, pipe additional rows of stars to fill the bottom red stripe of the flag. Fill the other two red stripes of the flag with piped icing, changing pouches of red as necessary. Fill the two stripes of white piped icing in the same manner using the white decorating icing pouch.

Lightly press the star cookie cutter into the tops of the nine set-aside cupcakes. If desired, fit the white icing pouch with a small round tip to pipe an outline around the stars. Then, fill in the stars by changing the tip to a medium star tip. Using a blue decorating icing pouch and medium star tip, fill in the remaining portion of each cupcake with blue piped icing, working it all the way to the outer edges. Place cupcakes back into the flag design and press gently together to join the blue frosted edges. Pipe additional blue icing into the joints and seams of the star portion of the cake.

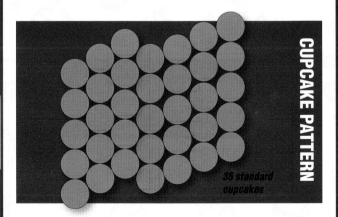

CUPCAKE PATTERN

35 standard cupcakes

Miss Daisy

You will need
- 14 x 18″ covered serving base
- Plastic piping bag with tips OR small plastic bag

Cupcakes
- 7 standard cupcakes, in white paper liners
- 13 mini cupcakes, in white paper liners
  Example used 1 (18.25 oz.) box mix, yielding 30 mini cupcakes and 12 standard cupcakes.

Frosting and décor
- 1 (16 oz.) container ready-to-use white frosting
- Green food coloring
- Green writing gel
- 1 (4.25 oz.) tube yellow decorating icing with tips
- 1 (6 oz.) pouch white decorating icing with tips

- 1 (4.25 oz.) tube red decorating icing
- 1 (4.25 oz.) tube black decorating icing with tips
- 1 piece black licorice, slivered thin

Directions

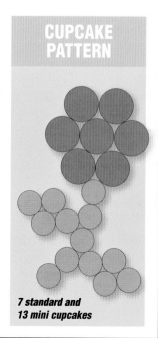

Arrange cooled cupcakes on serving base according to diagram. Use a small dab of frosting on the bottom of each mini cupcake liner to secure to base (stem and leaves). Pull cupcake petals away from the center temporarily.

Blend green food coloring into 1 cup of white frosting to reach desired shade. Smooth frosting over the entire stem and leaf portion of the cake, working to the edges to create a seamless appearance. Draw veins on the stem and leaves using green writing gel. If desired, pipe green edging around the stem and leaves, using a small round tip or a plastic bag.

Spread a thin layer of white decorating icing over each individual white petal cupcake; spread yellow decorating icing over the center cupcake. Place iced cupcakes back into flower shape. Fit white and yellow decorating icings with a medium star tip to create white rosettes on the petals and yellow rosettes on the center. Pipe an edge around each petal and the center, filling in crevices where petals adjoin.

To make the ladybug, squeeze the tube of red decorating icing (no tip), while holding steady, to create a large round dollop of icing. With a very small round tip or plastic bag (see hints on p. 8), pipe black icing onto the bug to create spots and lines as shown. To create eyes, pipe dots of black on top of larger dots of white. Poke the black licorice slivers into the ladybug to create antennae.

CUPCAKE PATTERN

7 standard and 13 mini cupcakes

Great Gumballs!

You will need

- 9″ round white-covered cardboard
- Bowl (or other round base) for height, approx. 1½ x 6½″
- 13 x 18″ covered serving base

Cupcakes

- 6 standard cupcakes, in white paper liners
- 30 mini cupcakes, in white paper liners
  Example used 1 (18.25 oz.) box mix, yielding
  12 standard and 36 mini cupcakes.

Frosting and décor

- 1 batch Royal Icing, recipe p. 58
- 1 (6 oz.) pouch red decorating icing
- Food coloring gels in pink, blue, green, yellow and orange
- 1 (4.25 oz.) tube black decorating icing with tips
- 1 chocolate wafer cookie, one edge sliced off, optional

Directions

Use a bread knife to slice one standard cupcake in half. Invert the bowl, top it with the cardboard and place it on serving base to create the surface for the mini cupcake "gumballs." Arrange cupcakes according to diagram; the edges of the standard cupcakes at the top and bottom of the gumball machine should be tucked slightly under the raised cardboard.

Divide Royal Icing equally between seven small dishes. Blend in coloring gel to make five colored icings. Leave one dish white. In the final dish, blend in black decorating icing sparingly to create dark gray. Set gray icing aside. Stir each of the six icings while adding drops of water to reach appropriate consistency; icing should not be runny, but thin enough to create a smooth finish when spread. Disassemble gumballs to spread five to six mini cupcakes with each color (except gray); set aside to dry.

Remove cardboard. Secure remaining standard cupcakes/halves to base with a dot of red icing. Smooth red icing over the machine base and top, spreading evenly to form an outlined edge. Mark the rectangular outline of the coin slot with a toothpick. Pipe black icing around the edge of coin slot, then dab gray icing into the center and use a toothpick to gently work it toward black edge. If desired, insert cookie wafer piece as coin slot crank, or allow gray icing to dry before piping on a black icing crank and round coin slot.

Gently place the cardboard back into position. Working from the center outward, place mini cupcakes on top of cardboard according to diagram; distribute colors evenly. Place remaining "gumballs" around edge of machine, setting them on their sides and gently lifting the cardboard enough to tuck mini cupcakes underneath as shown.

CUPCAKE PATTERN

*6 standard and
30 mini cupcakes*

Crazy Caterpillar

You will need

- 12 x 30″ covered serving base*
- Small plastic bag

Cupcakes

- 12 standard cupcakes, in white or bold-colored liners
  Example used 1 (18.25 oz.) box mix, yielding 22 to 24 cupcakes.

Frosting and décor

- Food coloring gels in yellow and neon green
- 1½ C. Bright-White Decorating Icing, recipe p. 58
- Approx. 4 oz. candy-coated chocolate minis or mini baking bits
- 1 (4.25 oz.) tube black decorating icing with tips
- 2 same-color small lollipops

Directions

Arrange eleven cooled cupcakes on serving base according to photo. Unwrap the remaining cupcake and cut a scant piece from one side. Stack the cut cupcake on top of an end cupcake, flat side down, as the head; set aside.

Variation: Use the extra cupcakes to make a second caterpillar for double the fun. Make them a couple by tinting one blue and one yellow; add curly eyelashes or thick eyebrows for added effect.

Blend coloring gels into white icing to create desired green color. Spread icing on individual body cupcakes, setting them apart from one another. Determine desired pattern for candies and gently press them onto each cupcake. If desired, pipe a green edge around the perimeter of each cupcake; spoon extra icing into a small plastic bag, smooth to one corner, twist the top of the bag and snip the corner for piping.

Place cupcakes back into caterpillar shape. Smooth a generous amount of icing over the caterpillar "head" created with the stacked cupcakes. Wisp icing into peaks to look like hair. Press two brown candies onto face, as eyes. Fit black decorating icing tube with a small round tip; pipe a smile onto the face. Press red candies onto mouth corners and reposition cupcake head. Insert lollipop antennae. Pipe black icing "legs" directly onto base beneath cupcakes. Place a dot of icing next to the bottom of each leg and press brown candies into dots to secure "feet."

*Plastic-coated white freezer paper makes a great base cover, especially when piping icing directly onto the surface. It is easy to wipe mistakes clean for a fresh start, if needed, and won't bleed or stain.

Hickory Dickory Dock

You will need
- 15″ to 16″ round base

Cupcakes
- 19 standard cupcakes, in decorative paper liners
  Example used Chocolate Buttermilk Cupcakes, recipe p. 56, yielding 24 standard cupcakes.

Frosting and décor
- 1 batch Marshmallow Buttercream Icing, recipe p. 56
- Food coloring gels in pink and orange (or colors coordinating with paper liners)
- 1 (4.25 oz.) tube black decorating icing with tips
- 2 Tootsie Rolls
- 3 Hershey's Kiss chocolates
- 3 maraschino cherries with stems
- 6 sliced almond pieces

- 1 oz. chocolate-flavored almond bark
- Black writing gel
- Red writing gel

Directions

Place the seven middle cupcakes on serving base according to the diagram; fasten in place with a dab of icing, if desired. Smooth approximately one cup of icing over them. Divide remaining icing equally between three small bowls. Set aside one bowl, uncolored; blend coloring gels into the two other bowls to create desired colors. Spread each colored icing onto six cupcakes, holding back a little of each color of icing for later use. Using a black decorating icing tube fitted with a small round tip, pipe even numbers 2 through 12 onto one color of cupcake and odd numbers 1 through 11 onto the other. Mark the eyes and mouth using a toothpick; pipe on black decorating icing as marked.

Fill a piping bag fitted with a small or medium star tip with remaining colored and white icings; do not completely blend the colors. Pipe a "tie-dye effect" icing edge around the perimeter of each cupcake. Set cupcakes into proper position on the serving base.

Roll Tootsie Rolls on a clean surface to shape into clock hands (2½" and 3" long); place on cake. Pat dry cherries and hold by the stems to dip and coat with melted almond bark; set on waxed paper to dry. Use barely melted bark to attach two almond slices to the flat side of each Kiss as mouse ears. Once head and body are set, use barely melted bark to attach Kiss and cherry; set on waxed paper to dry. Make writing gel dots as the black eyes and red nose. Place mice on cake and serving base.

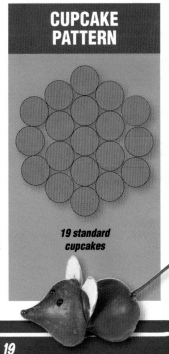

CUPCAKE PATTERN

19 standard cupcakes

Chicky Babes!

You will need

- 16 x 20″ covered serving base
- Small plastic bags
- Plastic piping bags with tips

Cupcakes

- 23 standard cupcakes, in paper liners
  *Example used 1 (18.25 oz.) box mix, yielding
  24 standard cupcakes.*

Frosting and décor

- 3½ C. white ready-to-use decorating icing*
- Food coloring gels in yellow and orange
- 1 (4.25 oz.) tube black decorating icing with tips

Directions

Place cooled cupcakes on serving base according to diagram. Add a dab of white icing to each cupcake bottom to secure it to the base. Divide and blend coloring gels into white icing to produce 2 cups of yellow and ¼ cup of orange; leave remainder white.

Spoon approximately ¼ cup of white icing and ¾ cup of yellow into separate piping bags fitted with medium star tips and set aside. Spread remaining white icing over the bottom two rows of cupcakes, smoothing it up onto the third row of cupcakes; leave the wings unfrosted and create a jagged pattern to resemble the cracked edge of an egg. Use remaining yellow icing to cover the rest of the cupcakes, smoothing it into the corners of the jagged white edge. Pipe a yellow border of stars around the chick and over the joint where yellow and white icing meet; pipe white icing stars along the bottom edge of the egg. Change the tip on the yellow piping bag to a large star tip. Squeeze small spirals of icing onto the chick's head and longer strokes of icing on the wings.

Divide orange icing evenly. Tint one half darker by blending in additional coloring gel and spoon it into a small plastic bag; twist the bag's top and snip off the corner. Use a toothpick to mark the location for the beak, then pipe dark orange around it. Use light orange icing to fill in the beak outline, spreading it with a toothpick.

Mark the location for the eyes using a toothpick. Fit the black tube of icing with a small round tip. Pipe icing to draw the eyes as shown. Squeeze white icing into the open portion of the eyes and spread with a toothpick.

A recipe for Bright-White Decorating Icing is on p. 58.

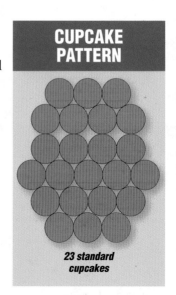

CUPCAKE PATTERN

23 standard cupcakes

Flutter By

You will need

- 16 x 20″ covered serving base
- Plastic piping bag with tips
- 2 (6″) lollipop sticks*

Cupcakes

- 27 standard cupcakes, in pastel paper liners
  *Example used 1 (18.25 oz.) box mix, yielding 27 cupcakes.***

Frosting and décor

- 4½ C. Bright-White Decorating Icing, recipe p. 58
- Food coloring gels in green, pink, yellow and purple
- 2 dark-colored decorating sprinkles, optional
- 1 candy necklace
- Edible clear glitter, optional

Directions

Arrange cooled cupcakes on serving base according to diagram. Spread them out slightly for ease during icing.

Blend food coloring gels into divided icing to make 1 cup green, 1 cup pink, 2 cups yellow and ½ cup purple. Place green icing in a piping bag fitted with a medium star tip. Pipe green icing onto five "body" cupcakes, starting at the very outer edges and working toward the centers. Change bags and tips as needed to pipe pink icing onto eight cupcakes for the bottom wings and yellow icing onto 14 cupcakes for the top wings.

Press the "body" cupcakes together in a line down the center of the board, and then bring the wings in toward the body, gently pressing them together for a more seamless look. If desired, fill joints with coordinating icing.

Fit a decorating bag with a small to medium round tip and pipe purple icing around the wings to outline them. Pipe purple eyes and mouth onto face. If desired, place dark sprinkles onto eyes for better definition. Use a large round tip to pipe purple spots onto the yellow wings. If desired, sprinkle pink sections of wings with edible clear glitter.

Cut the candy necklace apart to make candy beads. Slide approximately 20 candy beads onto lollipop sticks and bend them slightly. Just before serving, insert the empty end of the stick into the cupcake to create antennae.

*Plastic drinking straws can be used in place of lollipop sticks. Cut a straw in half lengthwise and then curl the pieces to slide candy beads on.

**Stretch your recipe or box mix to get 27 cupcakes or adjust upper outside wing pattern, if necessary.

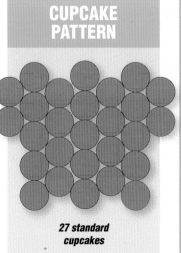

CUPCAKE PATTERN

27 standard cupcakes

Touchdown!

You will need
- 18 x 26″ covered serving base
- Plastic food wrap
- Parchment or freezer paper for a pattern, optional

Cupcakes
- 24 chocolate standard cupcakes, in red foil liners
  (or preferred team color)
- 10 jumbo cupcakes, in white paper baking cup liners
  *Example used 2 batches of Chocolate Buttermilk
  Cupcakes, recipe p. 56, yielding 24 standard and
  12 jumbo cupcakes.*

Frosting and décor
- 1 batch Chocolate Buttercream Icing, recipe p. 59
- 2 (4.25 oz.) tubes white decorating icing with tips
- 1 (4.25 oz.) tube red decorating icing with tips
  (or preferred team color)

Directions

Slice two standard cupcakes in half while in their foil liners. Arrange cupcakes on serving base according to diagram; fasten in place with a dab of icing, if desired. Carefully spread Chocolate Buttercream Icing across cupcakes, starting at the center and working toward the outside. For a seamless look, use extra icing where the taller jumbo cupcakes meet the shorter standard cupcakes. Smooth icing into a "straight" line around the outside cupcakes to form the football's edge. (These cupcakes are so yummy, they won't need frosting all the way to the outside of each cupcake!)

Create a "leathery" look by dabbing the icing surface lightly with a piece of crumpled plastic food wrap. If desired, create a paper pattern for the rounded lines on the football's ends (1¼″ wide) and the straight portion of the laces (also 1¼″ wide). Use the pattern pieces or work freehand to mark them with a toothpick. Fill each of the football's lines by piping three to four wide lines of white decorating icing directly from the tube and then smooth with a spatula. Use a toothpick to lightly mark the position for the eight laces. Pipe laces in place, again using white decorating icing with no tip.

If desired, create a paper pattern for the monogram. Use the pattern or work freehand to mark the letter in the icing, using a toothpick. Fit the white decorating icing tube with a small round tip and pipe the outline of the letter onto the cake. Fit the red decorating icing tube with a small star tip; pipe icing to fill the letter.

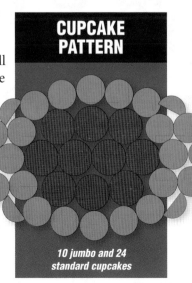

CUPCAKE PATTERN

10 jumbo and 24 standard cupcakes

Over the Rainbow

You will need

- 14 x 18″ covered serving base
- Plastic piping bags with tips

Cupcakes

- 38 standard cupcakes, in silver foil liners
  Example used 2 batches of Rainbow Cupcakes, recipe p. 57, yielding 40 cupcakes.

Frosting and décor

- 4 to 5 (16.2 oz.) containers fluffy white whipped frosting (approx. 10½ C.)
- Food coloring gels in red, yellow, green and blue (orange and violet, optional)

Directions

Place cooled cupcakes on serving base according to diagram. Once arranged, set the 14 cloud cupcakes aside while frosting the rainbow.

Spread one container of fluffy white frosting over the entire rainbow; allow frosting to sink into joints, making a smooth top surface. Use a toothpick to draw lines into the frosting to serve as a guide for adding rainbow colors.

Divide and color frosting with coloring gels as follows:

Red – 1½ C.	Green – ¾ C.
Orange – 1¼ C.	Blue – ½ C.
Yellow – 1 C.	Violet – ½ C.

Add gel gradually, but generously, to make bold colors. If only using four main colors, blend red and yellow gel to create orange and blend red and blue to create violet.

Fit a piping bag with a large round tip to pipe each frosting color in a zig-zag fashion onto the rainbow. Start with the red, followed by orange, yellow, green, blue and violet, as shown. Use remaining white frosting to cover the cloud cupcakes. Slide and gently press cloud cupcakes into position at the bottom edges of the rainbow.

TIP: *Whipped icing will not set up stiffly. If serving to small children, you may prefer to substitute decorator icing for less mess. Care should also be taken when serving heavily colored icings, which can stain clothing.*

CUPCAKE PATTERN

38 standard cupcakes

Fit for a Princess

You will need

- Serrated knife
- Rolling pin
- Plastic piping bag with tips
- 2 (8″) wooden or bamboo skewers
- Waxed paper
- 10 x 14″ covered serving base

Cupcakes

- 25 standard cupcakes, in pastel paper liners
  Example used 1 (18.25 oz.) box mix, yielding 25 cupcakes.*

Frosting and décor

- 6 sugar cones
- 6 (8″) lollipop sticks
- 3 oz. vanilla-flavored almond bark or candy coating
- 6 Laffy Taffy candies
- Food coloring gels in neon pink and neon orange
- Colorful decorating sprinkles (approx. 2 oz.)

- 4 C. white ready-to-use decorating icing**
- 1 (1 oz.) box candy conversation hearts, optional

Directions

Slice the tip from each cone with the knife to leave a hole just large enough for a lollipop stick. Melt almond bark according to package directions. Slowly add coloring gels to reach desired shade of pink. Spoon melted bark over each cone, smoothing off excess with the spoon as needed. Shake candy sprinkles over coating; set upright on waxed paper to dry.

Place each taffy piece between two layers of parchment paper and flatten with a rolling pin. Trim each piece into a flag shape, 1¼″ high and 2″ wide. Wrap the straight edge of the flag around the end of a lollipop stick. Set on waxed paper to harden.***

Arrange 14 cupcakes as castle base, according to diagram. With a piping bag and large star tip, pipe four wide zig-zag rows of icing over the top of castle base to cover. Pipe icing onto each remaining cupcake in a circular pattern. Stack one cupcake onto each corner of castle base. Make a short tower in the center area by stacking three cupcakes on top of the base; slide a skewer, sharp end first, down through the center of the entire stack. Make a taller tower using the same method and four cupcakes.

Slide flags into the cones' holes, standing them upright. Place one cone on top of each of the six stacks. Pipe additional icing around the base of each flag stick, if desired. Create a candy heart wall along the front and back of the castle, if desired.

*Stretch your recipe or box mix to yield 25 cupcakes. If preferred, adjust the height of one tower to use only 24 cupcakes total.

**A recipe for homemade Bright-White Decorating Icing is on p. 58.

***Fresh taffy may droop when flags are positioned upright. Allow taffy to harden into flag shape overnight, for best results.

CUPCAKE PATTERN

25 standard cupcakes

You will need

- Small plastic bags
- 15″ square covered serving base

Cupcakes

- 16 standard cupcakes, in white or green paper liners
  *Example used 1 (18.25 oz.) box mix, yielding
  22 round-topped cupcakes.*

Frosting and décor

- 6 (4.25 oz.) tubes decorating icing with tips
  (one each of black, red, yellow, blue, purple,
  orange and green)
- 1 (16 oz.) container white decorating icing*
- 15 white candy wafers

Directions

Set candy wafers on a clean work surface. Fit black
icing tube with a small round tip. Pipe each of the
numbers 1 through 15 onto the flat surface of a wafer;
set aside to dry.

Spread white icing on eight cupcakes; smooth it on neatly to create a rounded edge; set aside.

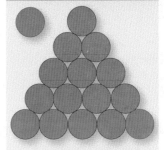

CUPCAKE PATTERN

16 standard cupcakes

Empty half of the red icing tube into a small bowl. Gradually add small amounts of black icing, stirring in between each addition, until desired "burnt red" color is reached. Spread one cupcake with each of the following colors and smooth on neatly to create a rounded edge: black, red, burnt red, yellow, blue, purple and orange.

To create the striped balls for each color (except black), mark the location for a 1¼″ wide stripe down the center of seven of the set-aside white frosted cupcakes (see string tip on p. 9). Pipe colored icing along the marked lines. (No decorating tip is required; squeeze each color directly from the tube except burnt red – spoon it into a plastic bag and snip a corner for piping (see tip on p. 8). Add one more line of icing down the center of each outlined stripe. Smooth out icing to make a neat ribbon of color across each cupcake.

Put a dot of icing on the bottom of each numbered candy wafer and place on cupcakes according to chart. Arrange cupcakes on base according to photo, leaving plain white cupcake to the side as cue ball.

	Solids	Stripes
Yellow	1	9
Blue	2	10
Red	3	11
Purple	4	12
Orange	5	13
Green	6	14
Burnt red	7	15
Black	8	–
White	Cue ball	–

Display Suggestion

Use green felt for the base to resemble a pool table. Add accessories to the cake display, such as small pool cues and a ball rack.

A recipe for Bright-White Decorating Icing is on p. 58.

Dino-mite!

You will need

- 14 x 18″ covered serving base
- Plastic food wrap
- Plastic piping bags with tips

Cupcakes

- 10 standard cupcakes, in decorative paper
  or foil liners
- 20 mini cupcakes, in decorative paper or foil liners
  *Example used 1 (18.25 oz.) box mix, yielding
  12 standard and 30 mini cupcakes.*

Frosting and décor

- 3½ C. white ready-to-use decorating icing*
- Food coloring gels in neon green, blue,
  orange and purple
- 1 (4.25 oz.) tube black decorating icing with tips

Directions

Place cooled cupcakes on serving base according to diagram. Add a small dab of icing to the bottom of each cupcake liner to secure it to the base. Divide icing and use coloring gels to create colors as follows: 1¾ cups green, ¾ cup blue, ½ cup orange, ¼ cup purple and ¼ cup white. Smooth green icing over the body, head and feet of the dinosaur as shown (using a little more than 1 cup). Create a rough appearance by dabbing the icing surface lightly with a piece of crumpled plastic food wrap.

Pipe orange spots onto the dinosaur and a squiggly line down the back, using a piping bag fitted with a medium round tip (or snip the corner of a filled plastic bag, see p. 8). Place blue icing into a plastic piping bag and pipe large "paws" along the bottom of each dinosaur leg using a large round tip. Change to a small round tip and squeeze in a random squiggle to create "hair" at the top of the head; add tiny dots to the orange spots.

Smooth blue icing to one side of the piping bag and fill the bag with remaining blue and green icing with one color on each side of the bag. Use a large round tip to pipe a green/blue edge around the bottom, sides and head of the dinosaur. Pipe a circular pattern of icing onto each scale (mini cupcakes) of the dinosaur's back.

With a small round tip, pipe black icing around the mouth and eyes. Fill the mouth and eyes with white piped icing. Pipe eyeballs and nostrils using black icing. Add purple icing with a small round tip to create spots and claws on top of the paws.

A recipe for Bright-White Decorating Icing is on p. 58.

CUPCAKE PATTERN

10 standard and 20 mini cupcakes

Leon Lion

You will need

- 14 x 18″ covered serving base
- Waxed paper
- Rolling pin
- Plastic piping bags with tips

Cupcakes

- 19 standard cupcakes, in decorative paper or foil liners
  *Example used 1 (18.25 oz.) box mix, yielding
  22 to 24 standard cupcakes.*

Frosting and décor

- ¾ batch Chocolate Buttercream Icing, recipe p. 59
- 1 batch Creamy Peanut Butter Icing, recipe p. 59
- 1 (4.25 oz.) tube black decorating icing with tips

Variation: A medium star tip can be used in place of a "grass" tip to create hair. Use the same procedure as described below. The cupcake shown here is an example of what star tip "hair" looks like.

Directions

Arrange cupcakes according to diagram; fasten in place with a dab of icing, if desired. Smooth peanut butter icing over lion face, spreading it just over the inside edge of the perimeter cupcakes (to help cover gaps). Smooth extra icing to form small round ears. Outside edge of peanut butter icing doesn't need to be perfect, as "hair" will cover the edges. Place a large piece of waxed paper over the lion's face and very gently roll over it with a rolling pin to create a smoother finish to the icing. Use a toothpick to draw the edge of lion's face (hairline); use it as a guide for piping "hair."

Fill a piping bag with Chocolate Buttercream Icing and fit it with a "grass" tip (example used Wilton #233). To pipe a small row of icing fringe along the outside edge of a pair of cupcakes squeeze icing from the bag, then lift as pressure is released from the bag and "lay" the icing toward the outside edge of the lion. Continue to pipe small rows along the first row, laying new hair over top of previous row until the hairline has been reached. Repeat process to complete hair by sections.

Mark facial features with a toothpick. Change the tip on the chocolate icing to a large round tip to pipe the top portion of the lion's nose; smooth any lines with a toothpick. Change to a medium round tip to make marks on the ears. Pipe black icing from the tube fitted with a small round tip to complete the facial features.

CUPCAKE PATTERN

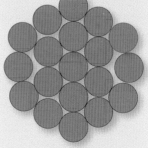

19 standard cupcakes

Blast Off!

You will need
- 18 x 26″ covered serving base
- Plastic piping bags with tips

Cupcakes
- 24 standard cupcakes, in silver foil liners
  *Example used 1 (18.25 oz.) box mix, yielding
  24 standard cupcakes.*

Frosting and décor
- 5 C. Bright-White Decorating Icing, recipe p. 58
- Food coloring gels in neon green, yellow,
  blue and purple

- White birthday candles
- Small frosted star-shaped sugar cookies, optional

Directions

Place cooled cupcakes on serving base according to diagram. Divide icing and use coloring gels to create colors as follows: 1¼ cups green, 1 cup yellow, 1¾ cups purple/blue and 1 cup white. Add a small dab of white icing to the bottom of each cupcake liner to secure it to the base.

Smooth green icing over the two center cupcakes at the base of the rocket and over the top nine cupcakes making up the tip portion of the rocket. Smooth yellow icing over the five remaining cupcakes at the center of the rocket. Smooth purple/blue icing over the outside supports of the rocket. Use photo as a guide.

Fill a piping bag with the purple/blue icing and fit it with a large star tip. Pipe two circles of icing onto the top green portion of the rocket ship, where the icing may have settled between cupcake joints. Pipe thick rows of purple/blue icing to cover the line where the yellow and green icing meet.

Fill a piping bag with white icing and fit it with a small star tip. Pipe a decorative border around the entire ship. Pipe white accents onto the ship in straight lines or in rows of stars as desired.

Insert birthday candles along the base of the rocket ship to represent the "fire" of blast-off. If desired, arrange star cookies on the base around the ship to create a night sky.

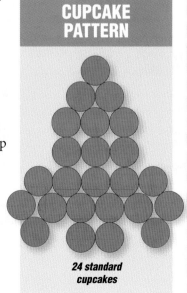

CUPCAKE PATTERN

24 standard cupcakes

Get Rolling!

You will need

- 16 x 20″ covered serving base

Cupcakes

- 2 jumbo cupcakes, in white paper liners
- 13½ standard cupcakes, in white paper liners
- 3 mini cupcakes, in white paper liners
  *Example used 1 (18.25 oz.) box mix, yielding
  2 jumbo, 14 standard and 10 mini cupcakes.*

Frosting and décor

- 2½ C. white ready-to-use decorating icing*
- 2 (4.25 oz.) tubes blue decorating icing with tips
- 1 (4.25 oz.) tube purple decorating icing with tips
- 1 (4.25 oz.) tube black decorating icing with tips

Directions

Slice one cupcake in half; one half will be used and the other can be set aside for another use. Slice the tops from two mini cupcakes to stack and use in the "boot" portion of the cake. Place cooled cupcakes on the covered serving base according to diagram, then set "wheels" and "toe-stop" aside. Add a small dab of white icing to the bottom of each boot cupcake liner to secure it to the base.

Ice each of the jumbo cupcakes with approximately 2 tablespoons of white icing. Spread the remainder of the icing over the surface of the "boot" portion of the cake. Smooth it toward the edges to create an outline that is as smooth/straight as possible.

Fit a blue icing tube with a medium star tip. Pipe small stars over the ankle, heel and toe portion of the boot, as shown. Remove the tip to pipe a thick stripe across the middle of the boot, directly from the tube. Pipe a purple stripe directly from the tube (with no tip) on each side of the blue stripe. With the same method, pipe a purple stripe around the outside of each white-iced wheel and set into position. After the stripes of icing have set up for a few minutes, gently press down along each piped line to flatten and widen slightly.

Squeeze about 1 teaspoon of black icing onto remaining mini cupcake, spreading it on evenly; place in toe-stop position. Fit the black icing tube with a small round tip to pipe lines on the wheels and laces on the boot.

*A recipe for Bright-White Decorating Icing is on p. 58.

Variation: Add initials or the name of the birthday person to the white portion of the skate, by piping from the extra icing in the black or blue tube. Change colors of the icing on the skate to their favorite colors for an even more personalized cake.

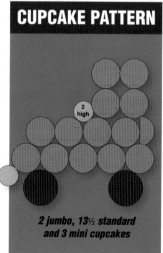

CUPCAKE PATTERN

2 high

2 jumbo, 13½ standard and 3 mini cupcakes

Sundae Best

You will need

- 16 x 22″ covered serving base
- Plastic piping bags with tips
- Small plastic bags

Cupcakes

- 6 jumbo cupcakes, in white paper liners
- 8 standard cupcakes, in white paper liners
- 4 mini cupcakes, in white paper liners
  *Example used 1 (18.25 oz.) box mix, yielding
  6 jumbo, 9 standard and 12 mini cupcakes*

Frosting and décor

- 1 (12 oz.) container whipped vanilla frosting
- ½ (12 oz.) container whipped chocolate frosting
- ½ (12 oz.) container whipped strawberry frosting

- 1 (4.25 oz.) tube black decorating icing with tip
- 1 (4.25 oz.) tube red decorating icing
- 2½″ piece of red peel-and-pull red licorice

Directions

Slice the top from one mini cupcake. Stack another mini cupcake on top of it for use as the "cherry." Place cooled cupcakes on serving base according to the diagram.

Place approximately ⅓ cup of vanilla frosting in a decorating bag fitted with an extra large star tip; set aside. Add a dab of vanilla frosting to the bottom of each cupcake that shapes the "sundae glass" to secure to base. Spread remaining vanilla frosting over the "glass" portion of cake, making edges smooth.

Pull jumbo cupcakes away from design to decorate. Spoon chocolate frosting into a plastic bag. Smooth frosting to one corner, twist the top of the bag and snip ¼″ to ⅜″ from the corner to create a round hole for piping. Start at the outside edge of one jumbo cupcake and pipe in a spiral motion to the center of the cupcake; repeat on two more jumbo cupcakes. Repeat method with strawberry frosting on two jumbo cupcakes. Place chocolate cupcakes along the top of the sundae glass; place strawberry ones above chocolate cupcakes.

With the piping bag of vanilla frosting, zig-zag icing randomly onto the last jumbo cupcake to look like whipped cream. Place on top of strawberry cupcakes.

Pipe black accent lines onto the sundae glass, using a small round tip. Squeeze a generous amount of red icing onto the mini "cherry" cupcake and smooth. Poke a hole into the cherry and gently push the licorice piece into the hole using a toothpick; place on top of "whipped cream."

CUPCAKE PATTERN

2 high

6 jumbo, 8 standard and 4 mini cupcakes

Flurries of Fun

You will need

- 18 x 26″ covered serving base
- Waxed paper
- Rolling pin
- Plastic piping bags with tips

Cupcakes

- 21 standard cupcakes, in silver foil liners
  Example used Vanilla Cupcakes, recipe p. 56,
  yielding 24 cupcakes.

Frosting and décor

- ½ batch Bright-White Decorating Icing, recipe p. 58
- White sparkling sugar sprinkles
- Food coloring gel (or paste) in sky blue
- Pearl or white large nonpareils

Directions

Place cooled cupcakes on serving base according to diagram; fasten in place with a dab of icing, if desired. Set aside approximately ¾ cup of white icing for later use. Thin remaining icing with drops of water, while beating, to make it easier to spread onto the cupcake cake. Divide thinned icing into thirds and spread one third on each set of cupcakes to create three snowflakes. Smooth it toward the edges to create smooth/straight outline.

To create a smooth icing surface before piping décor, cover each cake with a piece of waxed paper before it begins to harden. Then gently roll a rolling pin over the paper to create a smooth frosting surface. Carefully remove waxed paper and sprinkle sparkling sugar over each snowflake. Gently roll sugar into the icing in the same manner.

Slowly add and stir coloring into the reserved white icing to create a shade of very light blue. Spoon icing into a piping bag fitted with a medium round tip. Pipe lines of blue icing onto each set of white iced cupcakes to create the snowflakes. Embellish the snowflakes by adding pearl or white nonpareils.

Variation: For a large party, add more snowflakes to a larger base. Individualize the snowflake patterns for one-of-a-kind creations... just like the unique snowflakes found in nature.

Note: Some cake decorations appear to be edible, but are labeled "for decoration only." Always read and follow package labels carefully.

CUPCAKE PATTERN

7 standard cupcakes for each snowflake

Just Fir Fun

You will need

- 18 x 20″ covered serving base
- Plastic piping bags with tips
- 1½″ star-shaped candy mold (or purchased star candy)

Cupcakes

- 3 jumbo cupcakes, in white paper liners
- 13 standard cupcakes, in white paper liners
- 6 mini cupcakes in red, green and silver foil liners
  *Example used 1 (18.25 oz.) box mix, yielding
  3 jumbo, 15 standard and 8 mini cupcakes.*

Frosting and décor

- Candy wafers (yellow, red and navy blue)
- 2½ (16 oz.) containers ready-to-use white frosting
- ¾ C. powdered sugar
- ½ C. ready-to-use chocolate frosting
- Food coloring gels in green, yellow, blue and black

- 1 (4.25 oz.) tube red decorating icing
- 1 (4.25 oz.) tube white decorating icing with tips

Directions

To make yellow star, melt three yellow candy wafers in the microwave until smooth; spoon into star mold and chill until set.

Reserve ½ cup white frosting. Beat powdered sugar into remaining white frosting to thicken, then stir in green food coloring to desired shade. Arrange tree cupcakes on serving base according to diagram, omitting star and trunk. Fasten cupcakes in place with a dab of frosting, if desired. Smooth a layer of green frosting across cupcakes. Place remaining green frosting into a piping bag fitted with a medium star tip. Pipe a row of "pine branches" across the bottom edge of cupcakes, squeezing bag and lifting tip as pressure is released to "lay" frosting on cupcakes. Working from bottom to top of tree, pipe rows of frosting above the first row, laying some in opposing directions, until tree is covered.

Spread remaining jumbo cupcake with chocolate frosting, dragging a fork across the top to resemble tree bark (trunk). Frost one mini cupcake with white frosting; set candy star on top and place cupcake above tree. Divide remaining white frosting between three bowls. Leave one bowl white, tint one bowl navy blue and last bowl yellow. Spread red icing and colored frostings over mini cupcakes to make "gifts." Pipe frosting and icing "ribbons" and "bows" on gifts as desired.

Set trunk cupcake below tree; pipe on more green frosting to hide the seam. Pipe a garland on the tree with white decorating icing and a medium star tip. Decorate tree with colored candy wafers, flat sides up, or pipe on circles of colored icing. Place gifts under the tree.

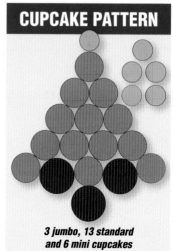

CUPCAKE PATTERN

3 jumbo, 13 standard and 6 mini cupcakes

Make a Fish Wish

You will need

- 18 x 26" covered serving base
- Small plastic bags

Cupcakes

- 4 standard cupcakes, in paper liners
- 62 mini cupcakes, in paper liners
  Example used 1 (18.25 oz.) box mix, yielding 72 mini and 4 standard cupcakes.

Frosting and décor

- 3 C. white ready-to-use decorating icing*
- Food coloring gels in blue, pink, green, purple and yellow
- 1 (3.5) oz. tube blue sparkle decorating gel; red and green, optional
- Sprinkles such as white sparkling sugar, tiny blue nonpareils, jumbo colored nonpareils**

Directions

Place cooled cupcakes on serving base according to diagram. Add a small dab of white icing to the bottom of each tailfin and face cupcake to secure it to base. Body/scale cupcakes should remain removable.

Place a tablespoon of white icing into a plastic bag; set aside. Divide remaining icing and use coloring gels to create colors as follows: 1 cup light blue, ¾ cup dark blue, ½ cup pink, ½ cup green, ½ cup purple, ¼ cup yellow; leave remainder white. Spread light blue icing onto the face and tailfin, smoothing the edges.

Decorate each mini cupcake to create a varied pattern of scales on the body of the fish. Some decorating methods can be performed with the cupcakes in position, but some will need to be removed, decorated and then set back in place. Create a unique look of your selection:

- Blue or purple icing swirled to look like scales
- Sparkle gel swirled or dotted on matching icing
- Iced, then dipped in sprinkles or tiny nonpareils
- Iced, then topped with jumbo colored nonpareils

Spoon yellow icing into a plastic bag. With yellow bag and reserved white bag, smooth icing to one corner, twist the top of the bag and snip off the corner to create a round hole. Pipe two lines of yellow icing to make a mouth. Pipe a white icing eye, and add a dot of blue sparkle gel to complete it. Use any remaining purple icing to make smooth accent lines on the tailfin and face.

*A recipe for Bright-White Decorating Icing is on p. 58.

**Nonpareils purchased in a container of rainbow colors may be separated into specific color groupings for a monochromatic look.

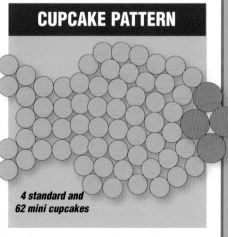

CUPCAKE PATTERN

4 standard and 62 mini cupcakes

47

Penguin Pal

You will need

- 16 x 20″ covered serving base
- Plastic piping bags with tips

Cupcakes

- 1 jumbo cupcake, in paper liner
- 12 standard cupcakes, in paper liners
- 6 mini cupcakes, in paper liners
  *Example used 1 (18.25 oz.) box mix, yielding
  4 jumbo, 12 standard and 12 mini cupcakes.*

Frosting and décor

- 1 (16 oz.) container white decorating icing*
- 1 (4.25 oz.) tube black decorating icing with tips
- 1 (4.25 oz.) tube pink decorating icing with tips
- 1 (4.25 oz.) tube orange decorating icing with tips
- 1 black licorice stick, optional

Directions

Place cooled cupcakes on serving base according to diagram; fasten standard cupcakes in place with a dab of icing, if desired. Fit the orange icing tube with a medium star tip. Pipe orange stars to cover the surface of each mini cupcake and set aside. Spread white icing over the jumbo cupcake, smooth evenly and set aside. Reserve 1 tablespoon of white icing. Spread remaining white icing over the entire body of the penguin and smooth evenly.

Using a toothpick, draw outlines into the white icing to mark the location for the black portion of the body and the scarf. Fit the black icing tube with a medium star tip and pipe stars around the outside of the body, leaving the belly white. Use a medium star tip with the pink icing tube to pipe icing for the scarf as shown. Add extra stars at the top of the scarf to create the dimension of a knot.

Using a toothpick, draw the outline of the face and the position for the eyes and beak on the jumbo cupcake. Pipe the eyes onto the cupcake using a small to medium round tip on the black icing tube. Pipe four dots to create a beak, using a medium round tip on the orange icing tube. Blend a dot of pink icing into the reserved tablespoon of white icing. Smooth a small amount of light pink icing onto each cheek, using the back of an offset spatula. Complete the penguin's head by piping medium stars from the black icing tube around edge.

Slide the head and feet into position. If desired, cut slivers of black licorice to insert into the head as a tuft of hair.

A recipe for Bright-White Decorating Icing is on p. 58.

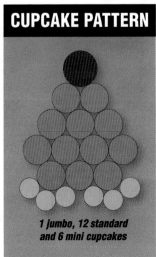

CUPCAKE PATTERN

1 jumbo, 12 standard and 6 mini cupcakes

Clowning Around

You will need

- 18 x 26″ covered serving base
- Parchment or freezer paper for a pattern, optional
- Plastic piping bag with tips

Cupcakes

- 5 jumbo cupcakes, in white paper liners, optional
- 7 standard cupcakes, in white paper liners
- 20 mini cupcakes, in white paper liners
  *Example used 1 (18.25 oz.) box mix, yielding
  5 jumbo, 7 standard and 24 mini cupcakes.*

Frosting and décor

- Approx. 5 C. white ready-to-use decorating icing*
- Food coloring gels in bright blue, neon green and yellow
- 1 (6 oz.) pouch red decorating icing with tips
- 1 (4.25 oz.) tube black decorating icing with tips

- Decorating sprinkles in blue, green, yellow and orange
- Pull-n-peel red licorice twists

Directions

Arrange cooled cupcakes according to diagram. Secure face cupcakes to the base with a dab of icing. Smooth 1 cup of white icing across the face to create a flat surface. If desired, use a paper pattern or freehand the clown's "make-up" outline onto face using a toothpick.

Blend coloring gels into divided icing to make 1 cup blue, 1 cup green and ⅔ cup yellow; leave remaining icing white. Place icing into separate piping bags. Use a large round tip on red icing to outline the nose and a small or medium tip on blue icing to outline cheeks, chin and eyes. Use a small star tip to fill in red nose and blue cheek, chin and eye outlines. Outline mouth in red with a small round tip. Fit the black icing tube with a small round tip to fill in mouth and eyes; switch to a small star tip to create eyebrows. Fill facial spaces with white icing and a small star tip; switch to a small round tip to make dots on the eyes.

Pipe colored icing onto jumbos using a large star tip. Pipe white icing onto each mini using a large round tip; add sprinkles. If desired, secure balloons, hair and bow tie to base with a dab of icing. Place licorice as balloon strings.

Spread green icing onto "tie" cupcakes. Continue to decorate "tie" with yellow icing as desired.

*A recipe for Bright-White Decorating Icing is on p. 58.

CUPCAKE PATTERN

7 standard and 20 mini cupcakes

Sum of All Cupcakes

You will need

- 16 x 20″ covered serving base
- Plastic piping bags with tips

Cupcakes

- 22½ standard cupcakes, in decorative paper liners
  *Example used 1 (18.25 oz.) box mix, yielding
  22 to 24 standard cupcakes.*

Frosting and décor

- 2 (1.74 oz.) bags of chocolate candy-coated
  peanuts, optional
- Approx. 5 cups white ready-to-use decorating icing*
- Food coloring gels in yellow, neon pink,
  neon purple and neon green
- Yellow nonpareils

Directions

Slice one cupcake in half; one piece will be used and the other one can be set aside for another use. Place cooled cupcakes on serving base according to diagram. Fill large gaps with candy to prevent icing from sinking down after it has been smoothed over the cake. Add a small dab of white icing to the bottom of each cupcake liner to secure it to the base.

Spread white icing (approximately 3 cups) over the entire cake surface. Smooth it toward the edges to create a smooth/straight outline of the number. Spoon remaining white icing into a piping bag fitted with a large star tip, and pipe a decorative border around the edges of the cake.

Blend coloring gels into divided icing to make ⅓ cup each of yellow, pink and purple, and ¼ cup of green. Pipe flowers onto the cake in clusters as desired, using piping bags fitted with large and medium flower blossom or star tips. Fill the centers of the flowers with a dot of yellow icing and carefully top with yellow nonpareils for a special effect. Fit the green piping bag with a small leaf tip to add green icing leaves to the flower clusters.

A recipe for Bright-White Decorating Icing is on p. 58.

Variation: *Five is just one of the digits that can be created with cupcakes. See the diagrams on the next few pages to design a cupcake cake with another single digit or use two digits to celebrate an anniversary, such as a 40th wedding anniversary or an 18th birthday party.*

22½ standard cupcakes

CUPCAKE PATTERN

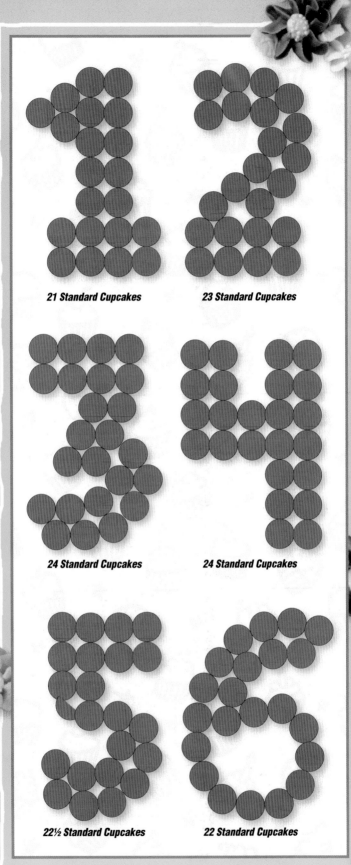

21 Standard Cupcakes

23 Standard Cupcakes

24 Standard Cupcakes

24 Standard Cupcakes

22½ Standard Cupcakes

22 Standard Cupcakes

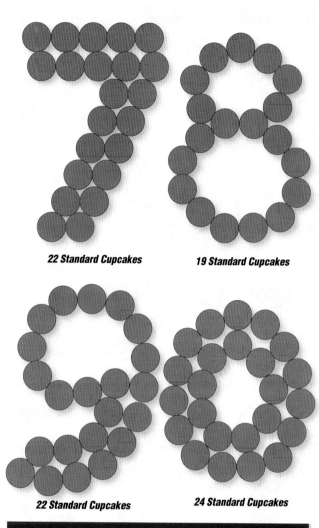

22 Standard Cupcakes

19 Standard Cupcakes

22 Standard Cupcakes

24 Standard Cupcakes

Design Your Own Cupcake Cake Creations!

View images in books, magazines or on the computer to develop ideas. Then cut paper circles to lay out as a pattern for the cake. Different-sized circles can be used to represent mini, standard and jumbo cupcakes (sizes listed on page 5). Once you know how many cupcakes of each size you need, you are well on your way to creating a one-of-a kind masterpiece.

Chocolate Buttermilk Cupcakes

Makes 24 standard or 12 jumbo cupcakes

2 C. flour
2 C. sugar
1 tsp. baking soda
¼ tsp. salt
1 C. butter

⅓ C. unsweetened cocoa powder
1 C. water
2 large eggs
½ C. buttermilk
1½ tsp. vanilla extract

Preheat oven to 350°F. In a large mixing bowl, combine flour, sugar, baking soda and salt; set aside. In a medium saucepan, combine butter, cocoa powder and water. Bring mixture just to boiling while stirring constantly. Remove from heat and add chocolate mixture to flour mixture; beat on medium speed until combined. Add eggs, buttermilk and vanilla; continue to beat for 1 minute. Pour batter into a muffin tin lined with paper baking cup liners. Bake standard cupcakes for 14 to 17 minutes (jumbos for 20 to 25 minutes) or until a wooden toothpick inserted in the center comes out clean. Cool on a wire rack before frosting.

Vanilla Cupcakes

Makes 24 to 28 standard cupcakes

1¾ C. cake flour (not self-rising)
1¼ C. flour
2 C. sugar
1 T. baking powder
¾ tsp. salt

1 C. unsalted butter, softened
4 eggs
1 C. whole milk
1 tsp. vanilla extract

Preheat oven to 325°F. In a large mixing bowl, combine cake flour, flour, sugar, baking powder and salt. Mix on low speed until well blended, about 3 minutes. Blend in butter, then add eggs one at a time, milk and vanilla; mix until combined. Spoon batter into baking cup liners, filling them about ⅔ full. Bake for 17 to 20 minutes or until a wooden toothpick inserted in the center comes out clean. Cool on a wire rack before frosting.

Note: *This recipe makes "flat-topped" cupcakes, which are very conducive to creating a level frosting surface for cupcake cakes.*

Rainbow Cupcakes

Makes 20 standard cupcakes

2 C. flour
1 T. baking powder
½ tsp. salt
4 eggs
1 C. sugar
1 C. vegetable oil

1 C. buttermilk
2 tsp. vanilla extract
Food coloring gels to
   make blue, green,
   yellow, orange and red

Preheat oven to 350°F. In a medium bowl, combine flour, baking powder and salt. In a large bowl, whisk together eggs, sugar, oil, buttermilk and vanilla. Add dry ingredients to large bowl and stir until just combined. Divide batter evenly between five small bowls; stir in food coloring gels until desired colors are reached. (To achieve rainbow colors, add plenty of coloring.)

Layer batter in muffin tins lined with 20 paper baking cup liners, by spooning an even amount of blue batter into the bottom of each cup, then repeating with green, then yellow, then orange and finally red batter. Each new color will not completely cover the previous color; do not attempt to spread them as they will spread nicely on their own, leaving a vibrant mix of colors inside. Bake for 15 minutes or until a wooden toothpick inserted in the center comes out clean. Cool on a wire rack before frosting.

Vanilla Cupcakes Royal Icing

Makes 3 cups

3 T. meringue powder
4 C. (approx. 1 lb.) sifted
   powdered sugar

6 T. warm water

Beat together meringue powder, powdered sugar and warm water for 7 to 10 minutes or until icing is smooth and forms peaks.

Marshmallow Buttercream Icing

Makes approx. 2¼ cups

1 C. butter, softened
1 (7 or 7.5 oz.) jar
   marshmallow creme

1⅓ C. powdered sugar
1 tsp. clear vanilla
   extract

In a medium mixing bowl, beat butter on medium speed until creamy. Add marshmallow creme and beat until well blended. Slowly add powdered sugar and vanilla, and gradually increase speed to high; beat for 3 to 4 minutes until fluffy.

Bright-White Decorating Icing

Makes approx. 7 cups

4 T. meringue powder
⅔ C. water + additional
   water
12 C. (approx. 3 lbs.)
   sifted powdered sugar
1¼ C. solid vegetable
   shortening

¾ tsp. clear vanilla
   extract
½ tsp. liquid butter
   flavoring
¾ tsp. salt

In a large mixing bowl, combine meringue powder and ⅔ cup water; whip on high speed until stiff peaks form. Reduce speed to low and add 4 cups powdered sugar, blending them in one cup at a time. Alternately add remaining powdered sugar and shortening. Add vanilla, butter flavoring and salt. Beat at low speed until smooth. If too stiff, add water, ½ teaspoon at a time, to reach desired consistency.

Chocolate Buttercream Icing

Makes approx. 3½ cups

½ C. solid vegetable
  shortening
½ C. butter
4 (1 oz.) squares
  unsweetened
  chocolate, melted

1 tsp. vanilla extract
4 C. (approx. 1 lb.) sifted
  powdered sugar
¼ C. milk

In a large mixing bowl, cream together shortening
and butter on high speed. Reduce speed and mix in
melted chocolate and vanilla. Add powdered sugar
one cup at a time; mixture will appear very dry. Blend
in milk and beat at medium speed until light and
fluffy.

Creamy Peanut Butter Icing

Makes approx. 1½ cups

¼ C. butter, softened
½ C. creamy peanut
  butter

1 C. powdered sugar
1 T. milk, additional
  if needed

In a medium mixing bowl, beat together butter
and peanut butter until well blended. Gradually
add powdered sugar, and as it begins to stiffen,
incorporate milk, beating until thick but spreadable.
Beat for a longer amount of time to make it fluffier.

Tips on Tips

Metal and plastic decorating tips can be purchased in different styles and sizes. Use tips to add designs and texture to your cupcake cakes with homemade or ready-to-use icings.

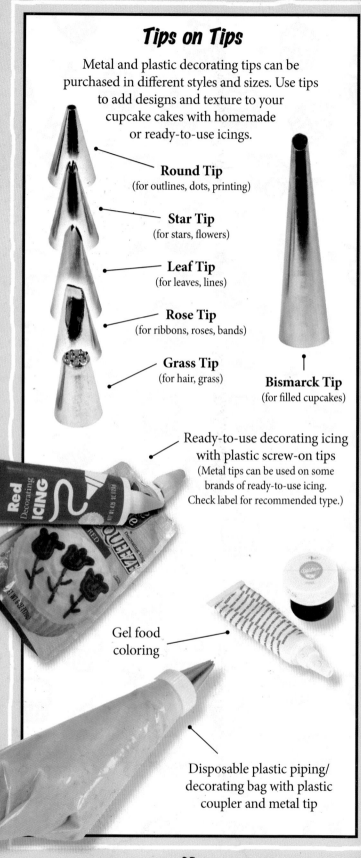

Round Tip
(for outlines, dots, printing)

Star Tip
(for stars, flowers)

Leaf Tip
(for leaves, lines)

Rose Tip
(for ribbons, roses, bands)

Grass Tip
(for hair, grass)

Bismarck Tip
(for filled cupcakes)

Ready-to-use decorating icing with plastic screw-on tips
(Metal tips can be used on some brands of ready-to-use icing. Check label for recommended type.)

Gel food coloring

Disposable plastic piping/decorating bag with plastic coupler and metal tip